FIGHTING FORCES ON THE SEA

DESTROYERS

LYNN M. STONE

Rourke
Publishing LLC
Vero Beach, Florida 32964

www.rourkepublishing.com

PHOTO CREDITS: title page, p. 5, 6, 8, 10, 13, 14, 15, 16, 28, 29 courtesy U.S. Navy; p. 18, 21, 23, 24, 27 courtesy Naval Institute; p. 22 courtesy U.S. Department of Defense National Archives

Title page: *A gunner's mate aboard the guided missile destroyer USS* John S. McCain *tests a Vertical Launch System (VLS) panel.*

Editor: Frank Sloan

Library of Congress Cataloging-in-Publication Data

Stone, Lynn M.
  Destroyers / Lynn M. Stone.
      p. cm. -- (Fighting forces on the sea)
  Includes bibliographical references and index.
  ISBN 1-59515-464-7 (hardcover)
  1. Destroyers (Warships)--Juvenile literature. I. Title. II. Series.

  V825.S76 2005
  623.825'4--dc22

2005014847

Printed in the USA

CG/CG

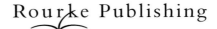

Rourke Publishing

www.rourkepublishing.com – sales@rourkepublishing.com
Post Office Box 3328, Vero Beach, FL 32964
1-800-394-7055

TABLE OF CONTENTS

CHAPTER ONE

★ DESTROYERS

The fleet, lightly armored U.S. Navy destroyers of World War II fame have evolved into far more deadly warships. The latest versions of American destroyers are, more accurately, guided missile destroyers of the *Arleigh Burke* **class**. The most recent of the *Burke*-class ships have more firepower per ton than any other type of ship in the world. They can travel independently or as part of warship battle groups.

The addition of guided missiles and other weaponry has changed the traditional, antisubmarine role of destroyers. *Arleigh Burke* destroyers can hunt submarines, but they are also designed and equipped to attack—or defend against—warships other than submarines, aircraft, **mines**, and on-shore threats.

▲
USS Benfold, *a guided missile destroyer in the* Burke *class, steams with the Japanese Defense Force destroyer* Kirisame *in a joint exercise of American and Japanese naval ships.*

▲

The guided missile destroyer USS Barry *cruises through the Arabian Sea. At the time of the photograph, in late 2004,* Barry *was part of the USS* Harry S. Truman *Carrier Strike Group.*

Arleigh Burke-class destroyers are loaded with computerized weapons systems. They give the destroyers greater accuracy in their choice and use of weapons. They also increase the ships' **survivability** in combat.

The Navy has 49 *Arleigh Burke*-class destroyers in service and 6 more have been ordered. Designated DDG warships by the Navy, *Burke* destroyers compose the largest group of surface warships in the Navy fleet. Size-wise, they are slightly smaller than guided missile **cruisers** and considerably larger than **frigates**.

▲

Flags waving, the guided missile destroyer USS Winston S. Churchill *dashes through the English Channel. The* Churchill *is the only active U.S. Navy vessel named for a foreign statesman.*

In addition to the *Burke* destroyers, the Navy has three *Spruance*-class destroyers (DD) in service, although they are being retired early this century. *Spruance*-class destroyers are longer, but they are not as wide or as heavy as the *Burke* destroyers. *Spruance*-class destroyers share the same type of **hull** as the Navy's *Ticonderoga*-class guided missile cruisers.

▲

With Burke-*class destroyers like the USS* Howard, *shown here on duty with a carrier strike group, the Navy returned to all-steel superstructures.*

The *Burke* design provided destroyers with greater armor by returning to all-steel construction. *Spruance* ships have steel hulls, but their **superstructures** are made of aluminum, a lighter metal.

The *Burke* destroyers were designed during the latter years of the Cold War (1945-1991) as fast, nimble, and heavily armed warships. The ships were to help counter the threat of the Soviet Union's naval weapons. In 1991, when the first of the *Burke*-class ships, USS *Arleigh Burke* (DDG 51), was **commissioned**, the long standoff between the United States and the Soviet Union was about to end. Nevertheless, the *Arleigh Burke*-class destroyers give the U.S. Navy an important hedge against any foreseeable threats on the seas.

Arleigh Burke class – DDG

Powerplant:
4 gas turbines, two shafts; 100,000 total shaft horsepower

Length:
511 feet (156 meters)

Beam:
59 feet (18 meters)

Displacement:
9,200 tons (8,506 metric tons), fully loaded (most recent ships, hulls #79 and higher)

Speed:
30+ knots (34.5+ miles, 55 kilometers per hour)

Aircraft:
LAMPS III electronics installed on landing deck for coordinating destroyer-and-helicopter antisubmarine operations; *Burke* hulls No. 79 and higher can carry as many as two helicopters

Ship's company:
23 officers, 300 enlisted

Armament:
Standard missiles, Harpoon missiles, ASROC (VLA) missiles; Tomahawk missiles; MK-46 torpedoes; 1 MK-45 5-inch (13-centimeter)/54-caliber lightweight gun; 2 Phalanx Close-In Weapons Systems

Commissioning date, first ship:
1991

▲

The Spruance-class USS Deyo *was photographed in 2003 during its mission in support of Operation Iraqi Freedom. The* Deyo *was among the U.S. warships to fire Tomahawk missiles at land targets in Iraq.*

DESTROYER CHARACTERISTICS

Weapons and how they operate help define a warship. The *Arleigh Burke*-class destroyers' range of missile types is itself impressive. But systems that trigger and deliver those missiles are just as impressive.

◀ *The guided missile destroyer USS* Milius *launches a Tomahawk Land Attack Missile toward Iraq early in the campaign to end the regime of Saddam Hussein.*

The guided missile destroyer The Sullivans *(foreground) joins with other American warships to launch a volley of missiles.*

Missiles aboard include the Standard, Harpoon, Vertical Launch ASROC (VLA), and Tomahawk. The Standard missile is an antiaircraft missile. The Harpoon is an anti-ship cruise missile. Tomahawks target land sites, even those beyond 1,000 miles (1,600 kilometers).

▲

In addition to missiles and the close-in 20-millimeter guns of the Phalanx system, the Spruance-class USS O'Bannon *has a .51-caliber MK-45 gun.*

The Vertical Launching System (VLS) on the destroyers can fire a mix of missiles. The VLS interfaces with the ships' Aegis Integrated Weapons System. Using a phased-array **radar** system called SPY-1D, Aegis automatically detects and tracks targets. Aegis can track and provide missile guidance functions for over 100 targets at once. And for the destroyer's traditional antisubmarine mission, the *Burke* class has an AN/SQQ-89 integrated antisubmarine warfare suite. It is the most advanced antisubmarine warfare system in the world. The *Arleigh Burke* destroyers also have long-range **sonar** instruments.

The ships' Phalanx Close-In-Weapons Systems, built around automated 20-millimeter guns, will eventually be replaced by Sea Sparrow missiles.

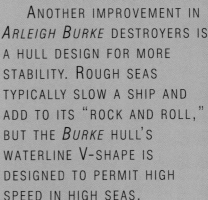

FACT FILE ★

ANOTHER IMPROVEMENT IN *ARLEIGH BURKE* DESTROYERS IS A HULL DESIGN FOR MORE STABILITY. ROUGH SEAS TYPICALLY SLOW A SHIP AND ADD TO ITS "ROCK AND ROLL," BUT THE *BURKE* HULL'S WATERLINE V-SHAPE IS DESIGNED TO PERMIT HIGH SPEED IN HIGH SEAS.

CHAPTER THREE

Torpedoes and the little, gnat-like torpedo boats that began to fire them in the 1890s gave birth to the destroyer. Basically, the destroyer was created to destroy torpedo boats.

The U.S. Navy floated its first destroyer, the USS *Bainbridge*, in 1901. The *Bainbridge* was essentially a torpedo boat destroyer. In future years, as the mission of destroyers evolved, the ships were simply called destroyers.

▲

The USS Bainbridge, *shown here in Asian waters in 1915 or 1916, became America's first destroyer when it was commissioned in 1901.*

American destroyer design and purpose had changed by the outbreak of World War I (1914-1918). These new destroyers served as escort vessels and submarine hunters when the United States entered World War I in April, 1917. American destroyers sank only one enemy submarine, the German *U-58,* during the war. But destroyers helped keep submarine wolf packs away from merchant ships and troopships traveling to Europe.

After the war, international treaties curbed production of large warships. But in the 1930s, the rise of Nazi Germany and Japan's conquest of China began to awaken the sleepy American warship industry.

FACT FILE ★

THE NAVY'S FIRST DESTROYER, THE USS *BAINBRIDGE*, WAS 250 FEET (76 METERS) LONG (CURRENT DDG SHIPS ARE 511 FEET [156 METERS] IN LENGTH) AND HAD A CREW OF 73 (DDGS HAVE A CREW OF 323). IT HAD A SPEED OF 29 KNOTS (33.4 MILES, 53 KILOMETERS) PER HOUR, REMARKABLY CLOSE TO A DDG'S 30-PLUS KNOTS.

CHAPTER FOUR

★ WORLD WAR II

U.S. destroyer forces served in World War II (1939-1945) from the beaches of Europe to the Aleutian Islands of Alaska and the tropics of the Pacific. More than 400 U.S. destroyers helped in the successful Allied war effort.

The widely used American *Fletcher*-class destroyers were typical of the era. They were nearly 377 feet (115 meters) long and just 39 feet (12 meters) wide. Armed with deck guns and torpedoes, they had a top speed of about 35 knots (40 miles, 64 kilometers per hour) and a crew of 329. They were the fastest of the large American warships.

A painting by Arthur Beaumont shows the Fletcher-class USS Charles Ausburne *leading Destroyer Squadron 23 during World War II.*

Using sonar for detection and **depth charges** for attack, American destroyers were important in antisubmarine warfare. But destroyers performed many tasks. Their antiaircraft guns helped defend larger warships, especially aircraft carriers, against Japanese warplanes. On April 6, 1945, for example, American destroyers *Bush* and *Colhoun* shot down several Japanese planes as they attacked U.S. aircraft carriers. Ultimately, Japanese ***kamikaze*** planes that escaped the antiaircraft fire dived into the destroyers, sinking them. A dozen destroyers were sunk by *kamikazes* in the closing months of World War II.

◀ *A depth charge explodes behind the stern of an American destroyer.*

The USS Johnston *was one of the American destroyers that faced an overwhelming Japanese naval force off Samar in October, 1944. The* Johnston *was eventually battered by Japanese fire and sank.*

Destroyers frequently dueled with enemy ships, too. In one such clash, Captain Arleigh Burke's destroyer squadron, without loss, sank three Japanese destroyers on November 11, 1943. And in one of the most heroic actions in U.S. naval history, 3 American destroyers and 3 destroyer escort ships charged into a flotilla of 23 Japanese warships, including 4 battleships, off Samar in October, 1944.

The selfless courage of the American crews and attacks by American carrier-based planes convinced the Japanese that they were facing a much larger, stronger force. Two American destroyers, a destroyer escort, and a carrier escort were sunk by Japanese fire. The Japanese fleet, also bloodied, retreated.

A painting by Dwight Shepler shows the USS Emmons *bombarding German positions in Normandy, France, on D-Day, June 6, 1944. The* Emmons *was later sunk by Japanese kamikaze planes in the Pacific Ocean on April 7, 1945.*

Destroyers bombarded shore targets, too. On June 6, 1944, famously remembered as D-Day, American destroyers in the company of hundreds of Allied warships blasted German positions on the shores of Normandy, France.

Life aboard a destroyer was extremely hazardous. Other than the risks posed by the enemy, destroyers faced collisions and angry seas. A typhoon sank three destroyers with the loss of 765 of their crews in December, 1944. The USS *Borie*, damaged after ramming the German **U-Boat** *405*, sank a day later. By war's end, 71 American destroyers and hundreds of their sailors had been lost.

CHAPTER FIVE

During the Korean War (1950-1953) and in the Vietnam War (1957-1975), American destroyers saw limited service, largely in patrol and intercept missions. But because of the ongoing Cold War with the Soviet Union, the United States continued to upgrade its destroyer forces. The *Charles F. Adams* class in 1959 introduced the first American guided missile destroyers. In 1975, the USS *Spruance* became the first gas-turbine powered U.S. destroyer.

Jack Vogelman's painting shows the guided missile destroyer USS Decatur, *one of the 1960s-era warships that saw duty in Vietnam.*

CHAPTER SIX

THE FUTURE OF DESTROYERS

Arleigh Burke-class destroyers will be around well into the 21st century. As the newest *Burke* ships are constructed, they are updated with advanced weaponry and technology as it becomes available. Meanwhile, the Navy is planning the next generation of destroyers, designated DD(X). These ships will be heavier than current destroyers, yet more difficult for enemy radar to detect because of their **stealth**-based hull design.

◀ *An SH-60B Seahawk helicopter lifts off from the guided missile destroyer USS* Mason *(DDG 87). The latest* Burke-*class destroyers, like the* Mason, *can carry two Seahawks.*

Weaponry will feature the Advanced Gun System, which can accurately fire shells against land targets up to 115 miles (185 kilometers) away. A new vertical launch system will expand the types of missiles that can be fired from a single launcher.

Driven by advanced technology and weaponry, DD(X) and other next-generation warships will continue to keep U.S. Navy supremacy on the seas.

▲

The new-generation DD(X) destroyer may look very much like this one drawn by an artist for the Navy. The DD(X) design shows a 689-foot (210-meter) long ship, considerably longer than the current Burke class ships.

GLOSSARY

class (KLAS) — a group of ships manufactured to the same, or very similar, specifications, such as the *Arleigh Burke* class of American guided missile destroyers

commissioned (kuh MISH und) — to have officially been placed into service by the U.S. Navy

cruisers (KRU zurz) — guided missile-carrying warships, the modern versions being slightly larger than, but similar to, guided missile destroyers

depth charges (DEPTH CHARJ uz) — undersea explosives commonly dropped by destroyers in attempts to sink submarines during World War II

frigates (FRIG utz) — surface warships, smaller than cruisers and destroyers, armed with guided missiles

hull (HUL) — the sides, bottom, and deck of a ship; the main, enclosing body

kamikaze (KAH muh KAH zee) — Japanese pilots who crashed their warplanes into American ships in 1944 and 1945

mines (MYNZ) — explosive devices generally planted on or near the ocean surface and triggered when struck by a ship

radar (RAY DAR) — a system based on sound echoes to detect the presence of distant flying objects

sonar (SOH NAR) — a system based on sound echoes to detect the presence of undersea objects

stealth (STELTH) — the name given to both ships and aircraft that have certain features that make them difficult to be detected by radar

superstructures (SOO pur STRUK churz) — the major structures built onto and rising above a ship's upper deck

survivability (sur VYV uh BIL uh tee) — the ability to survive; in the case of a ship, to stay afloat and operational

U-boat (YEW BOT) — the English term for the German word *Unterseeboote*, meaning undersea boat or submarine

INDEX

FURTHER READING

Green, Michael and Gladys. *Destroyers: The Arleigh Burke Class*. Edge Books, 2004

Green, Michael. *Destroyers*. Scholastic, 1998

WEBSITES TO VISIT

http://www.chinfo.navy.mil/navpalib/ships/destroyers
http://navysite.de/destroyers.htm

ABOUT THE AUTHOR

Lynn M. Stone is the author and photographer of many children's books. Lynn is a former teacher who travels worldwide to pursue his varied interests.